WHY SHOULD I RECYCLE?

ISBN 0-439-86640-5

First edition for the United States and Canada published in 2005 by
Barron's Educational Series, Inc. Copyright © 2002 by Hodder Wayland.
All rights reserved. Published by Scholastic Inc., 557 Broadway, New York, NY 10012, by
arrangement with Barron's Educational Series, Inc. SCHOLASTIC and associated logos
are trademarks and/or registered trademarks of Scholastic Inc.

12 11 10 9 8 7 6 5 4 3 2 1   6 7 8 9 10 11/0
Printed in the U.S.A.   23

First Scholastic printing, March 2006

WHY SHOULD I RECYCLE?

Written by Jen Green

Illustrated by Mike Gordon

SCHOLASTIC INC.
New York   Toronto   London   Auckland   Sydney
Mexico City   New Delhi   Hong Kong   Buenos Aires

In my family, we recycle our garbage. We return things so they can be used again.

We didn't always recycle.
We used to throw everything away!

On our way to school, we always pass Mr. Jones's house. Mr. Jones is our teacher.

One day, we saw him putting
a special box with cans, bottles,
and papers by the gate.

"This box is for recycling. All these things are taken away and used again," said Mr. Jones.

9

Mr. Jones said garbage contained lots of useful things that can be recycled, or used again.

Mr. Jones took the class to a recycling center. It had separate containers for bottles, cans, plastic, clothes, and paper.

12

"What do you think happens to all the glass that goes in here?" asked Mr. Jones.

"It all gets broken down to make new shiny bottles!

And guess what happens to all the cans that go in here?" asked Mr. Jones.

"They get melted down to make new metal things such as bikes and scooters.

Wow!

And what about the paper and plastic that goes in here, and here?" Mr. Jones asked.

"The paper gets shredded and used to make new books and comics.

This plastic can be used to make all kinds of things, including clothes. You might be wearing some!" said Mr. Jones.

"Most of the garbage we put in the trash can gets buried in dumps that spoil the countryside. It's good to recycle as much as you can!" said Mr. Jones.

"Clothes, books, and toys that you don't want can all be taken to the secondhand store," explained Mr. Jones.

I told Mom and Dad about our trip to the recycling center. Now we buy recycled things at the stores.

We also recycle everything at home. Fruit and vegetable peelings get recycled on our new compost heap.

The compost helps my Mom's prize vegetables to grow!

Now we recycle so much garbage, there's hardly any left to put in the can!

Recycling is kind to nature.
It saves money – and it's fun!

Notes for parents and teachers

Why Should I?

There are four titles about the environment in the *Why Should I?* series: *Why Should I: Save Water? Save Energy? Protect Nature?* and *Recycle?* These books will help young readers to think about simple environmental issues, and other social and moral dilemmas they may come across in everyday life. The books will help children to understand environmental change and how to recognize it in their own surroundings, and also help them to discover how their environment may be improved and sustained. Thinking about recycling will also teach children to consider others and to act unselfishly.

Why Should I Recycle? explains about the importance of recycling. It includes a number of tasks children can carry out to begin recycling themselves.

Suggestions for reading the book with children

As you read the book with children, you may find it helpful to stop and discuss issues as they come up in the text. Children might like to reread the story, taking on the role of different characters. Which character reflects their own attitude to recycling most closely? How are their own ideas different from those expressed in the book?

The book explains what happens to the materials that we recycle. Most of the garbage we put in the trash is packaging made from precious resources – paper and cardboard from trees, plastic from oil, glass, and cans from minerals from the ground. All these materials are then processed to make packaging, which uses energy and also creates pollution. Recycling helps us conserve precious materials and save energy, and so makes for a more sustainable future.

The book also introduces the problem of waste disposal and the damage it causes to the environment. Some of the vast amounts of garbage we throw away is burned in incinerators that pollute the atmosphere; the rest is buried in landfill sites that may pollute water supplies and land. Much modern waste does not rot, but remains intact for years. Recycling cuts down on waste disposal and thus helps to reduce pollution and save land.

Discussing the subject of recycling may introduce children to a number of unfamiliar words, including energy, environment, incinerator, landfill, packaging, pollution, refuse, and rot. Make a list of all the new words and discuss what they mean.

Suggestions for follow-up activities

Discuss facilities for recycling in your local area. Are there recycling centers nearby? If a recycling program exists locally, does your family make use of it? Some people assume that recycling is time-consuming and annoying, but in fact, it takes very little time. Children could find out how garbage needs to be sorted for local programs, and whether glass and cans need to be cleaned in preparation.

Encourage children to monitor the amount of waste that gets thrown away at home or at school each week. They could do a survey to find out what things are being thrown away, then begin to sift out materials that can be recycled. The book contains many suggestions for recycling. What other ideas can children come up with? Finally, they might like to monitor the reduction in waste in the garbage can once recycling is underway.

Books to read

Amos, Janine. *Pollution*. Orlando, FL: Steck-Vaughn, 1993.
Describes the ways in which our air, water, and soil are being polluted.

Bailey, Donna. *What We Can Do About Conserving Energy*. New York: Franklin Watts, 1992.
Identifies energy conservation issues and gives possible solutions for families and local groups.

Bellamy, David J. *How Green Are You?* New York: Crown Books, 1991.
Provides information and projects about ecology that teach children and their families how to conserve energy, protect wildlife, and reduce pollution.

Berenstain, Stan, and Jan Berenstain. *Berenstain Bears Don't Pollute (Anymore)*. New York: Random House, 1991.
The bears form the Earthsavers Club to teach others how to stop polluting and protect natural resources.

Dorros, Arthur. *Follow the Water from Brook to Ocean*. New York: HarperCollins, 1993.
Follows water from rainfall on the roof to the ocean and explains how important it is to keep our water clean.

Gibbons, Gail. *Recycle! A Handbook for Kids*. New York: Little, Brown & Company, 1996.
Explains the process of recycling from start to finish, focusing on five types of garbage, and describing what happens to each when it is recycled.